The Inside-Outside Book of
TEXAS

Roxie Munro

SeaStar Books
New York

Route 92, Big Thicket National Preserve

SEASTAR BOOKS
A division of NORTH-SOUTH BOOKS INC.

Library of Congress Cataloging-in-Publication Data
is available.
First published in the United States by SeaStar Books,
a division of North-South Books Inc., New York.
Published simultaneously in Canada by North-South Books, an
imprint of Nord-Süd Verlag AG, Gossau Zürich, Switzerland.

The art for this book was prepared using watercolor
and inks. The text for this book is set in Phoenix Chunky.

ISBN 1-58717-050-7 • TB • 10 9 8 7 6 5 4 3 2 1
ISBN 1-58717-051-5 • LB • 10 9 8 7 6 5 4 3 2 1

Printed in Italy

For more information about our books, and the authors and
artists who create them, visit our web site:
www.northsouth.com

To my mother,
Margaret Bissey Munro,
who misses the wide open spaces
of her West Texas childhood

—R. M.

Route 285, Reeves County

Dallas

Palo Duro Canyon

And inside

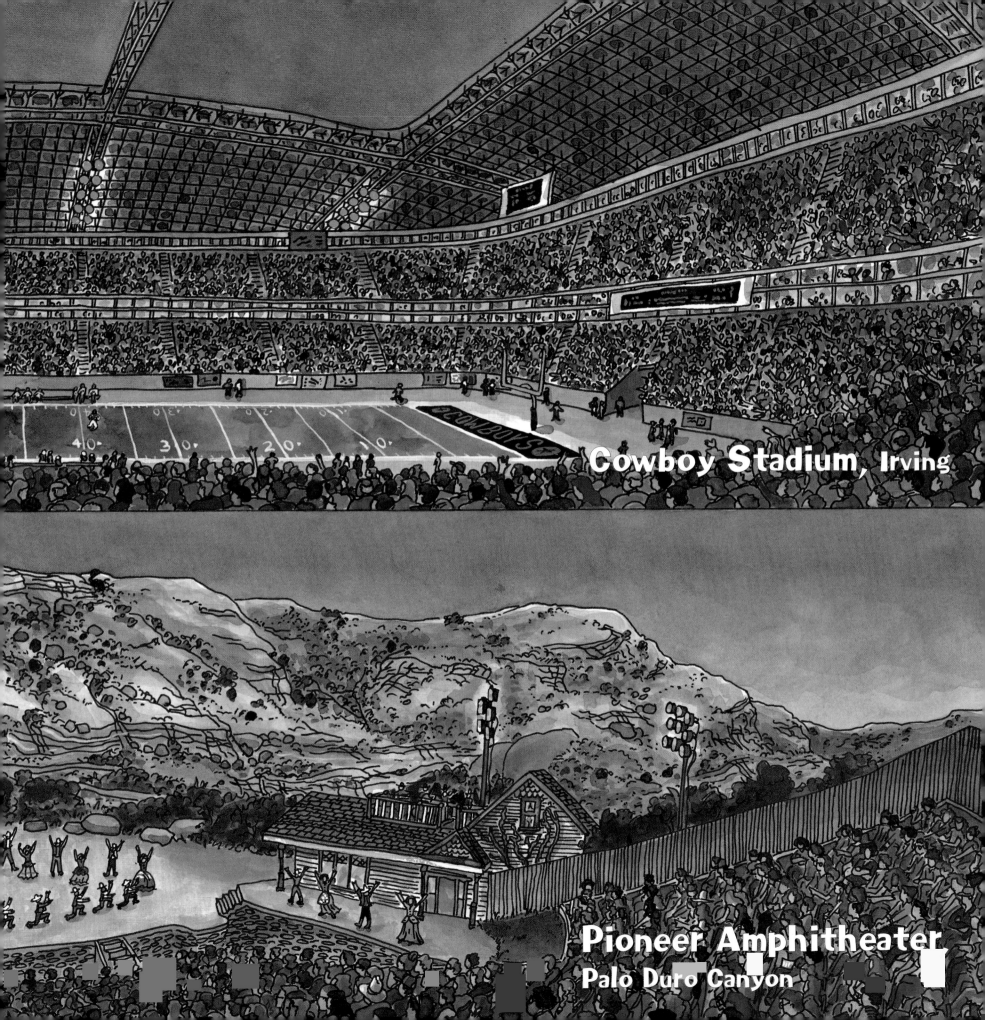

Cowboy Stadium, Irving

Pioneer Amphitheater
Palo Duro Canyon

Ranching

At Lambshead Ranch,
Albany

In the corral

In the cookshack

Cowboy hats

And boots

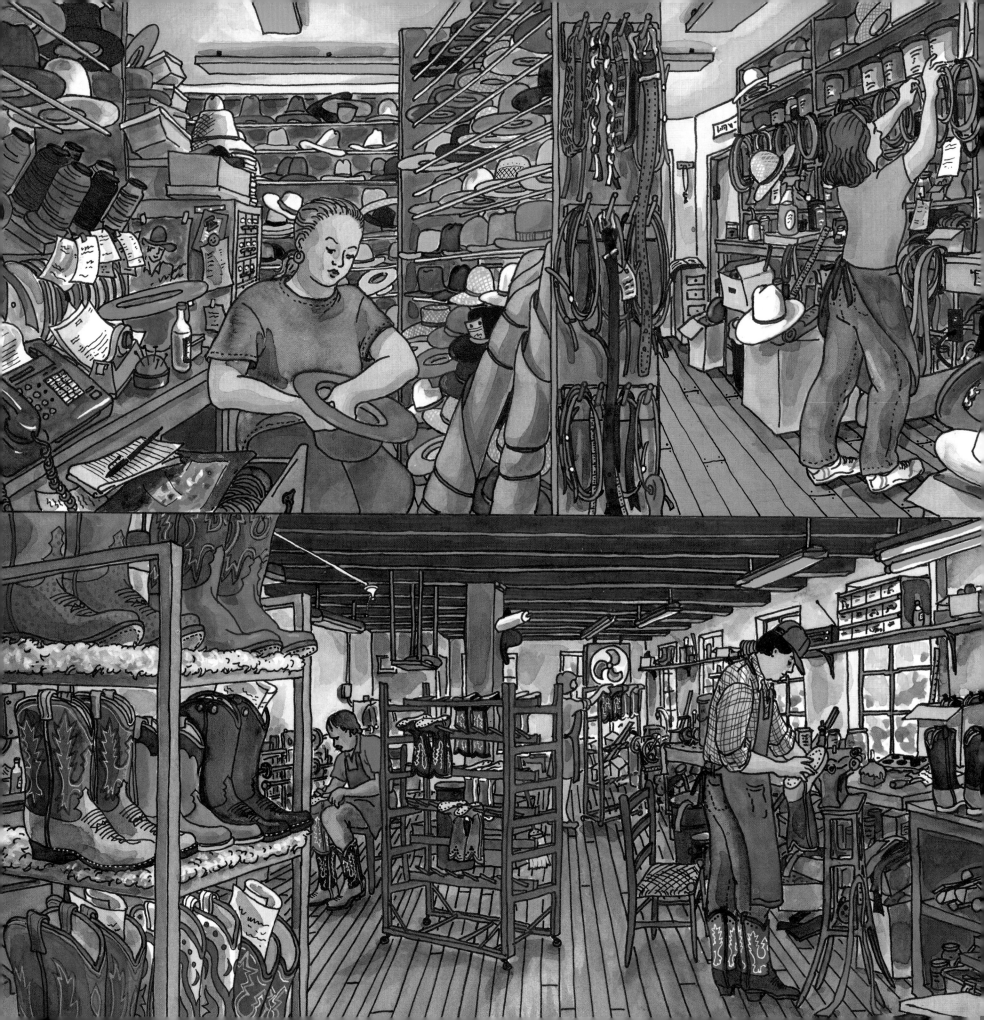

At Texas Hatters, Buda

At J. L. Mercer, San Angelo

Museums, outside . . .

Alamo Museum, San Antonio

Forestry Museum, Lufkin

Kimbell Art Museum, Fort Worth

Antique Sewing Machine Museum, Arlington

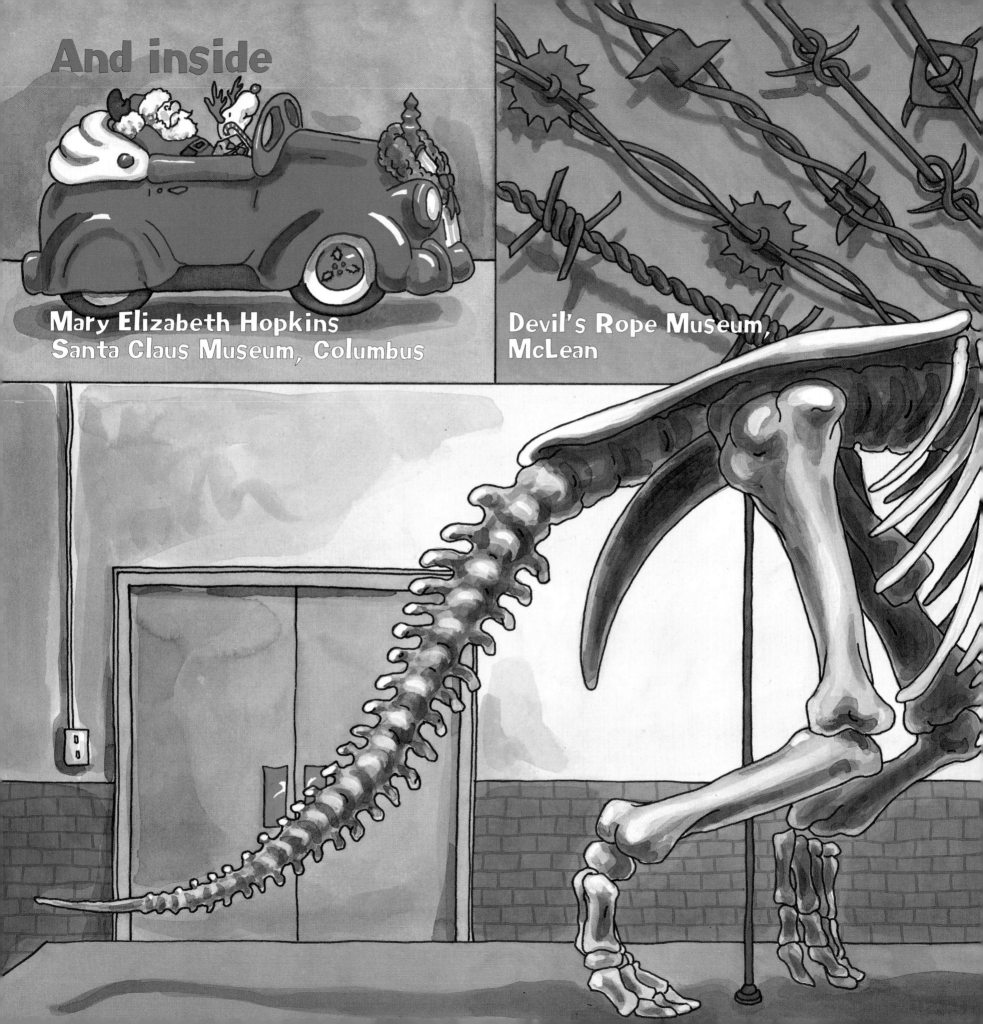

And inside

Mary Elizabeth Hopkins
Santa Claus Museum, Columbus

Devil's Rope Museum,
McLean

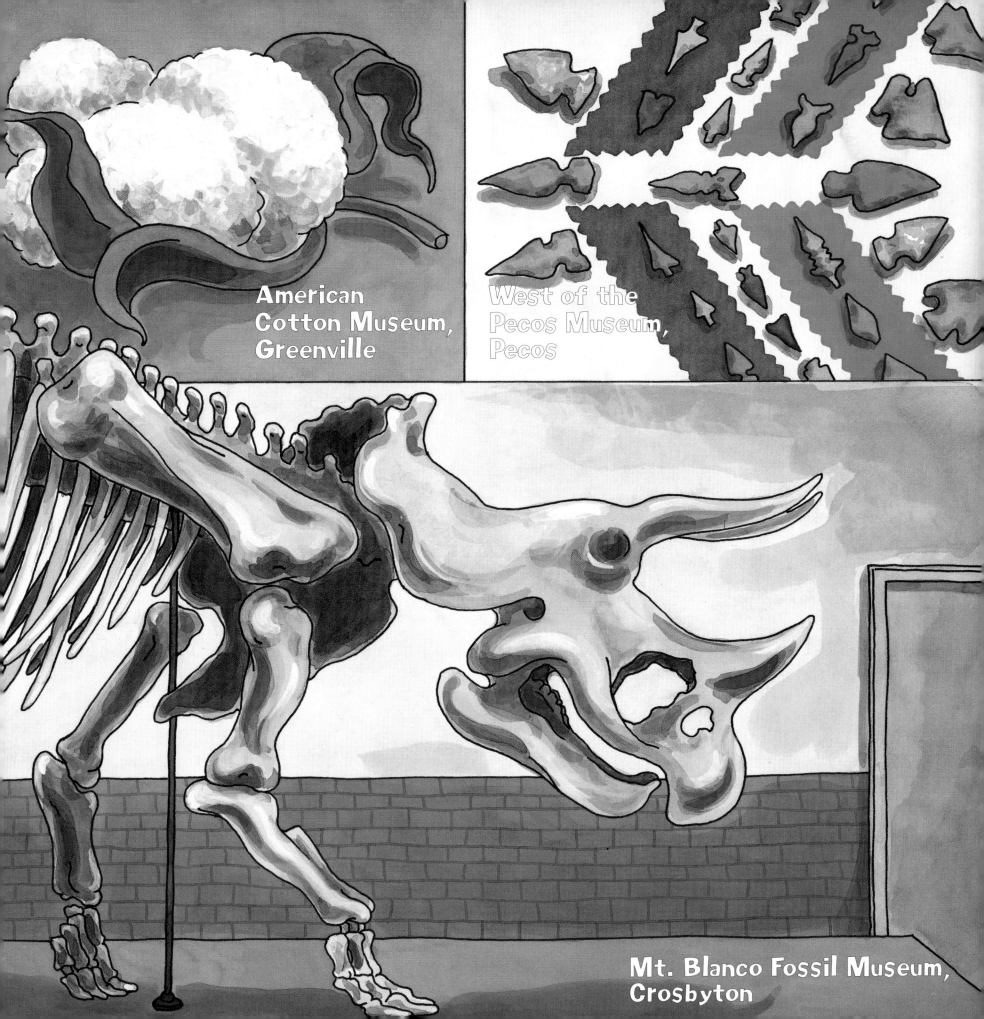

American Cotton Museum, Greenville

West of the Pecos Museum, Pecos

Mt. Blanco Fossil Museum, Crosbyton

Lyndon B. Johnson Space Center, Houston

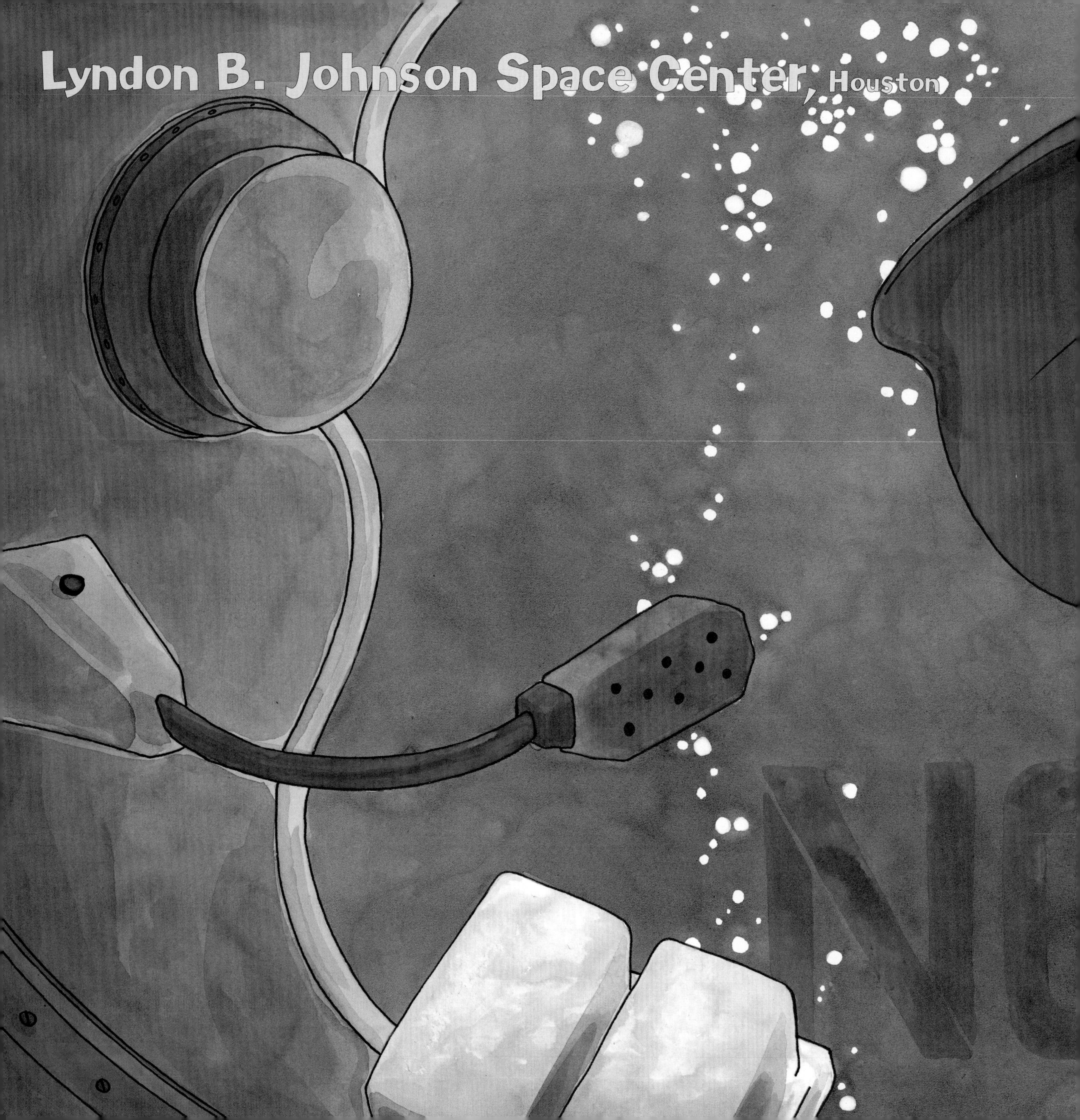

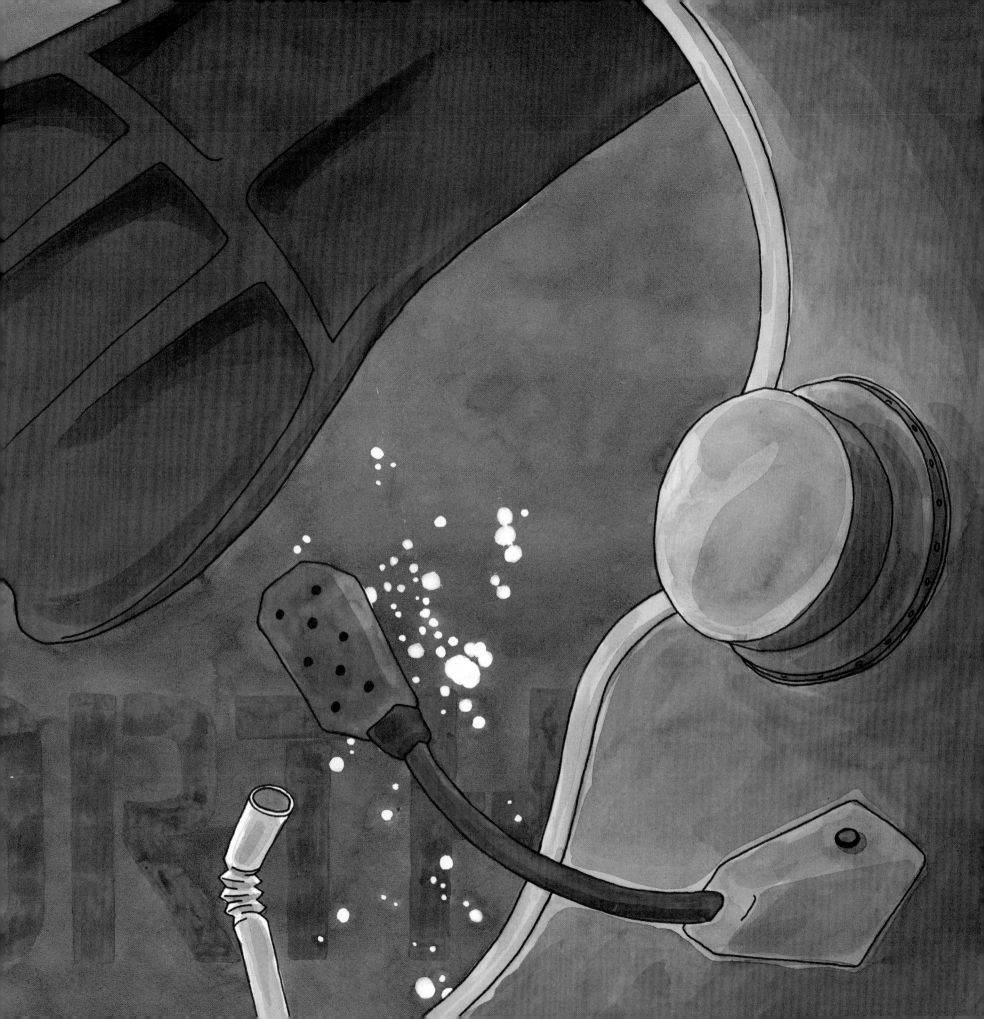

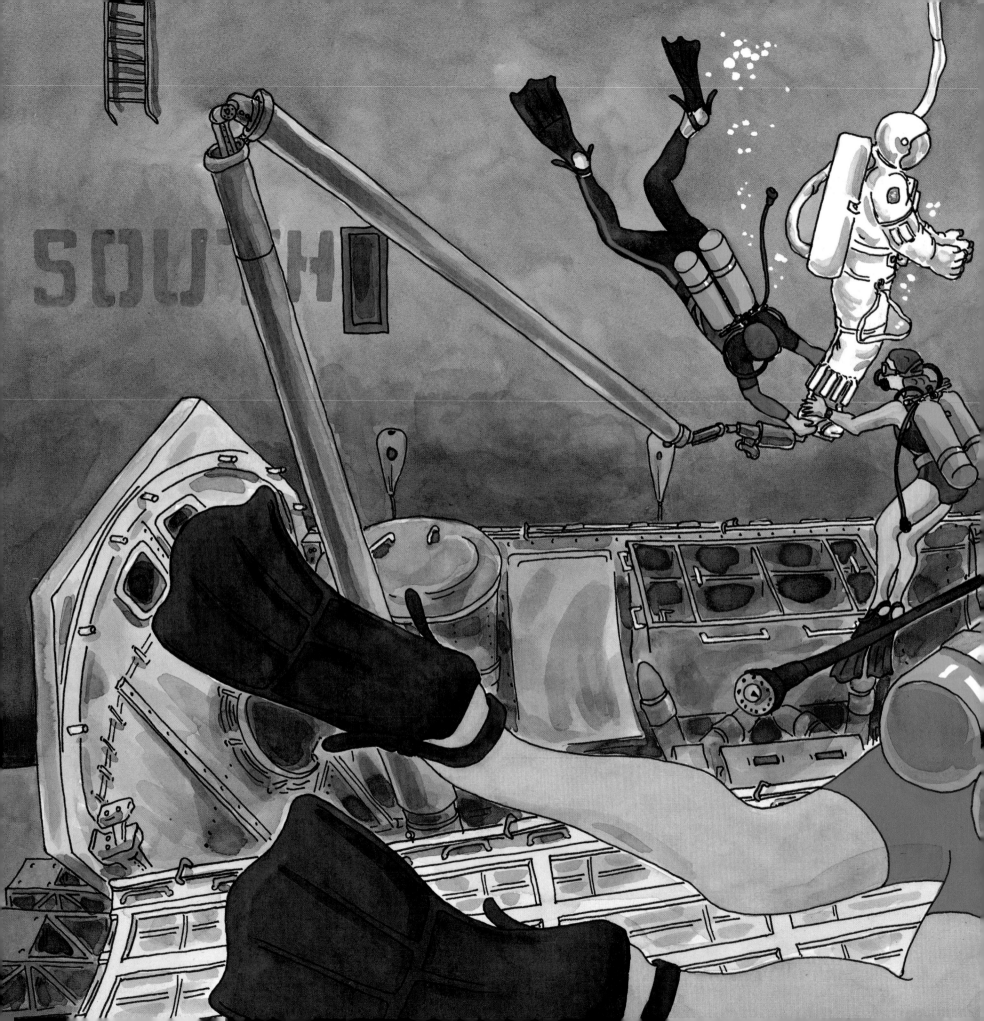

At the Neutral Buoyancy Laboratory

Oil

In Odessa

In Port Arthur

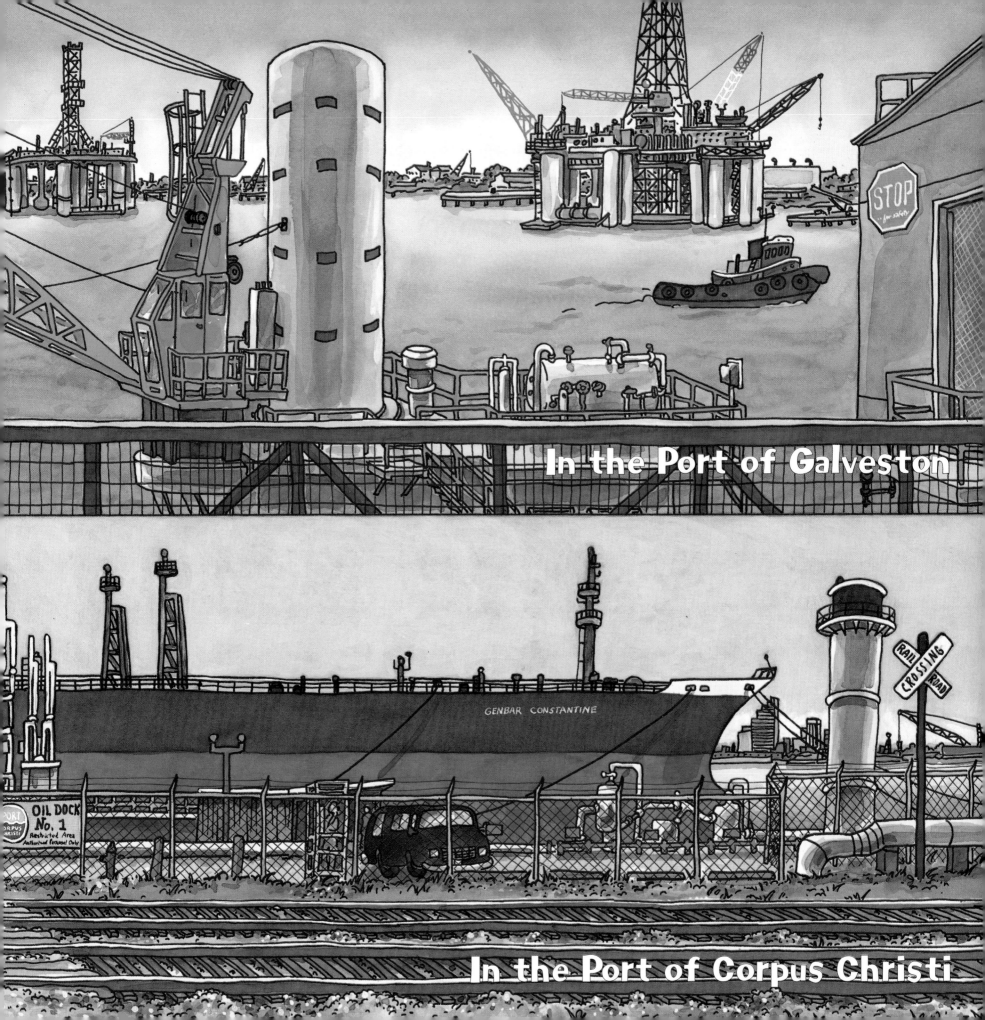

In the Port of Galveston

In the Port of Corpus Christi

In Port Isabel

On the River Walk, San Antonio

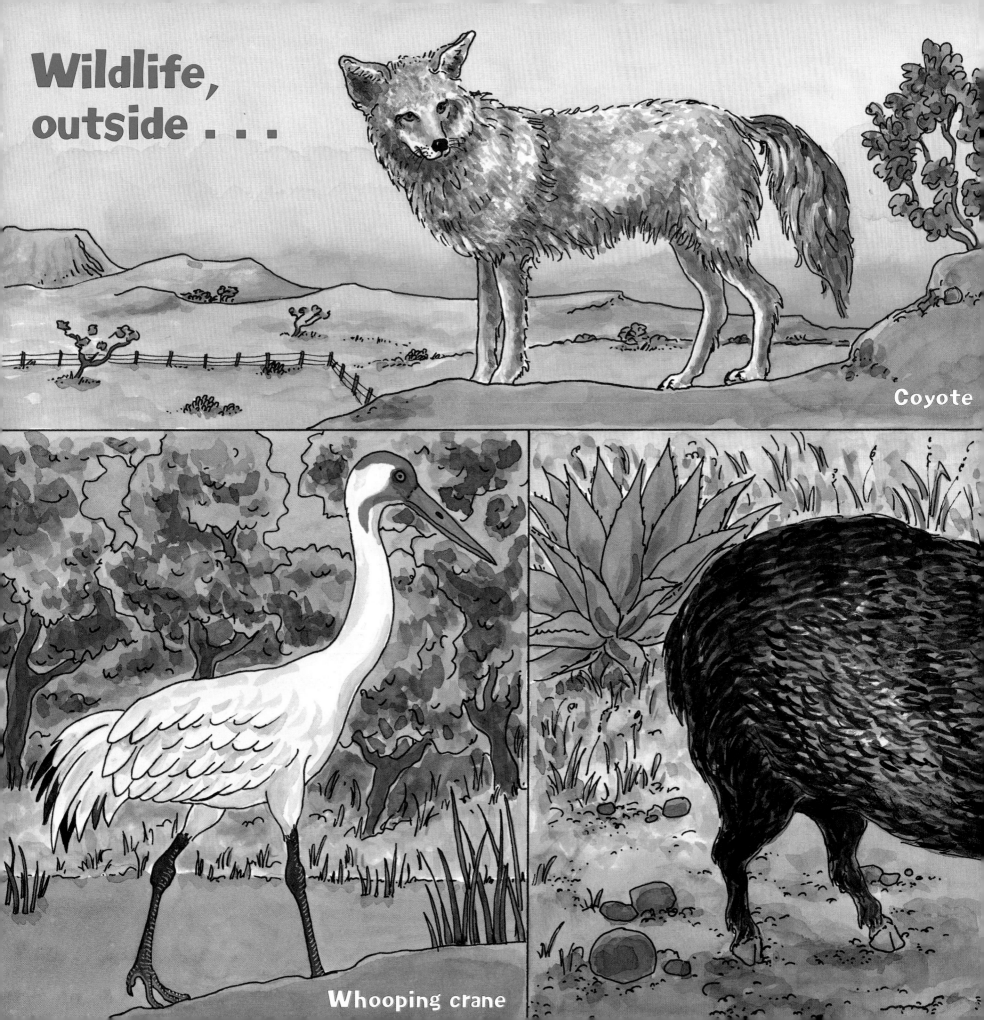

Wildlife, outside . . .

Coyote

Whooping crane

Roadrunner

Jackrabbit

Javelina

Tarantula

Cactus wren

Kangaroo rat

Trap-door spider

And inside

Mexican free-tailed bat

Alligator

American bittern

The Rio Grande

El Camino del Rio

And in El Paso

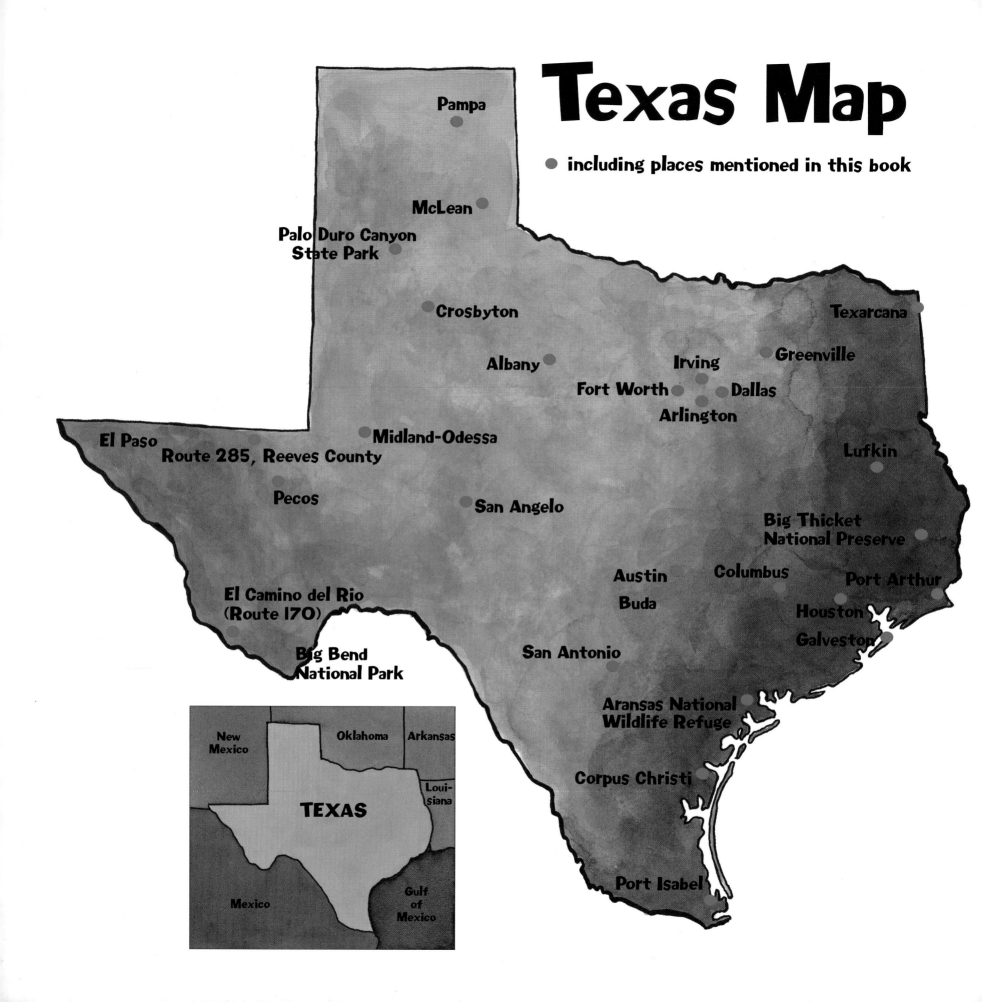

Texas Map

● including places mentioned in this book

Pampa

McLean

Palo Duro Canyon
State Park

Crosbyton

Texarcana

Albany

Irving

Greenville

Fort Worth

Dallas

Arlington

El Paso

Midland-Odessa

Route 285, Reeves County

Lufkin

Pecos

San Angelo

Big Thicket
National Preserve

Columbus

Austin

Port Arthur

El Camino del Rio
(Route 170)

Buda

Houston

Galveston

Big Bend
National Park

San Antonio

Aransas National
Wildlife Refuge

Corpus Christi

New
Mexico

Oklahoma

Arkansas

Loui-
siana

TEXAS

Mexico

Gulf
of
Mexico

Port Isabel

An Inside Look
at What's in This Book

State Tree:
PECAN

State Seal:
INCLUDES FIVE-POINTED
"LONE STAR"

TOP OF TEXAS RODEO, PAMPA The first American rodeo was held in Pecos, Texas, in 1883. It all started when two cowhands in a saloon, squabbling about who was the better roper and rider, decided to "have it out" in a competition outside. Now rodeo is the official sport of Texas, as well as part of the curriculum in many colleges and universities. The front and back covers show saddle bronc riding, an event in which the rider must stay atop the animal for at least eight seconds.

BIG THICKET NATIONAL PRESERVE Covering some 90,000 acres in East Texas, the Big Thicket National Preserve is a protected area where hardwood forests of the East, coastal wetlands, western prairies, and arid land of the Southwest all converge. Divided into eight separate land units and four river and stream corridors, it contains eighty-three species of trees, more than sixty kinds of shrubs, and nearly 1,000 flowering plants—nine of which are carnivorous. Animal life includes coyotes, gray foxes, bobcats, beavers, armadillos, and alligators, not to mention over two hundred species of birds.

ROUTE 285, REEVES COUNTY Texas is big—bigger than any European country. Distances are mind-boggling; it's farther from Texarcana to El Paso than it is from El Paso to Los Angeles. Nowhere can the state's immensity be felt more strongly than in West Texas. Route 285 seems to stretch forever through sparsely populated Reeves County.

State Small Mammal:
ARMADILLO

DALLAS Dallas is world famous, and not only because of a once-popular TV series with that name. It is known as the "Cadillac of Texas towns" and the "Manhattan of the Southwest." At dusk, the Dallas skyline is dazzling. Of the many landmark buildings that gleam in the light of the setting sun, Reunion Tower is one of the most recognizable, with its sphere on top of a fifty-story shaft.

Texas Stadium, Irving Home of the Dallas Cowboys, Texas Stadium in Irving (near Dallas) has a roof that stays open year-round. More than 65,000 fans fill the grandstands, while 15,000 more are treated to luxury suites—381 in all.

PALO DURO CANYON STATE PARK On the high plains in the Texas Panhandle, about an hour's drive from Amarillo, lies the incredible Palo Duro Canyon, an 800-foot-deep gorge formed by the Red River. It extends some sixty miles, featuring towering cliffs layered with bands of brilliant colors.

Pioneer Amphitheater A 600-foot cliff serves as the kaleidoscopic backdrop for *Texas*, a musical performed every summer at the outdoor Pioneer Amphitheater in Palo Duro Canyon State Park. The drama takes the audience back to the Panhandle of the Old West. A story of humor, hardship, and progress, it is full of spirited dancing and great visual effects, including riders spotlighted on cliff trails and ranchers battling a prairie fire.

RANCHING Texas has some 16 million cattle, more than twice as many as any other state. It leads the nation in livestock production and boasts the largest number of farms and ranches.

State Capitol:
AUSTIN

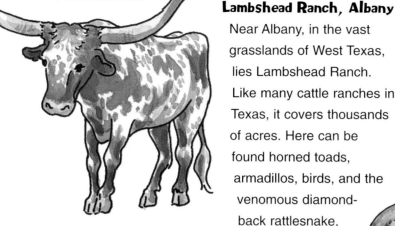

**State Large Mammal:
TEXAS LONGHORN**

**State Bird:
MOCKINGBIRD**

Lambshead Ranch, Albany

Near Albany, in the vast grasslands of West Texas, lies Lambshead Ranch. Like many cattle ranches in Texas, it covers thousands of acres. Here can be found horned toads, armadillos, birds, and the venomous diamond-back rattlesnake, among numerous other snakes and spiders. The mesquite tree, or "Texas ironwood," is used for fence posts, for furniture, and for smoking food. The prickly pear cactus, "the Devil's pincushion," is a constant problem for cowboys and their horses.

Corral Rounding up cattle is part of the job for cowboys working at the ranch. These cattle are hardy Texas longhorns, originally brought to North America by the conquistadors. A longhorn steer can stand six feet high at the shoulder and have a seven-foot horn spread.

Cookshack The cookshack is the business and social center of the ranch, with two fireplaces and a commercial kitchen. To cowboys, lunch is the big meal of the day. Sometimes other cowboys, sent by neighboring ranches to help out with work, join them here.

**State Dish:
CHILI**

COWBOY HATS AND BOOTS In Texas, hats and boots are often works of art, proudly worn not only by cowboys, but by Texans from all walks of life.

Texas Hatters, Buda "Big or Small . . . We Top Them All" is the motto of this famous establishment, where hats are made by hand. Over the years, there have been a number of notable takers, such as Bob Dylan, Willie Nelson, Prince Charles, and three American presidents.

J. L. Mercer & Sons Boots, San Angelo Customized boots have been made at family-run J. L. Mercer since it opened in 1923. A workforce of ten ensures that each boot is beautifully tooled, whether fashioned of plain cowhide or a fancier material. They have even made boots from ostrich, alligator, lizard, shark, and water buffalo skin!

MUSEUMS Texas has more than six hundred museums. Some are among the country's most lavish; many are unique, delightful, and even quirky.

The Alamo, San Antonio Originally a Spanish mission, the Alamo is the fort in which 189 brave defenders, vastly outnumbered by Mexican troops, held out for thirteen days in 1836. Symbolic of Texas's fight for independence, it is now a national shrine that includes a museum.

**State Stone:
PETRIFIED
PALMWOOD**

Kimbell Museum, Fort Worth Innovative use of natural light gives a contemporary edge to the presentation of fine art at the Kimbell Museum. Along with collections of Asian and African art, the museum is filled with the works of such masters as Rembrandt, Picasso, El Greco, Monet, and Cézanne.

Forestry Museum, Lufkin Deep in the Piney Woods of East Texas lies the Texas Forestry Museum. Among the exhibits is an old logging train with locomotive, log loader, log car, and caboose.

Antique Sewing Machine Museum, Arlington A giant working model of a sewing machine marks the entrance to America's first Antique Sewing Machine Museum in Arlington. On display inside, in a homelike setting, are 155 sewing machines that date from 1852 to the 1960s. On one of these century-old antiques, children can practice sewing in just the same way their great-great-great-grandmothers might have done.

Mary Elizabeth Hopkins Santa Claus Museum, Columbus The bright red car with Santa Claus at the wheel is one of more than two thousand Santa exhibits in this museum. Warmth, nostalgia, and Christmas songs fill a cozy home in which collectibles have been gathered from just about everywhere—including the German-made doll the museum's creator received in 1913, when she was six months old.

**State Flower:
BLUEBONNET**

Devil's Rope Museum, McLean Barbed wire, introduced in Texas around 1870, helped protect crops from wild buffalo and free-grazing cattle. "Historians believe that barbed wire and the windmill were as important in taming the West as the Winchester and six-gun," according to folks at the Devil's Rope Museum, where samples of every conceivable style of barb are on display.

**State Plant:
PRICKLY PEAR CACTUS**

American Cotton Museum, Greenville Visitors to Greenville, in an area known for its cotton industry, can go to this museum to learn about planting, growing, ginning, baling, spinning, and weaving of Texas's leading crop.

West of the Pecos Museum, Pecos Jumanos Indian arrowheads are some of the artifacts and mementos here that celebrate the vibrant past of Pecos, a city said to be the roughest town in the Old West. The museum occupies an old saloon and three floors of a historic hotel.

**State Fish:
GUADALUPE BASS**

Mt. Blanco Fossil Museum, Crosbyton On proud display stands a teenage triceratops, a cast reproduced from original bones. These ancient creatures had heads up to ten feet long, the longest of any known land animal. The museum also features a number of fossils found in Texas, such as giant salamander skulls and a skeleton of a mammoth dug up in Waco.

LYNDON B. JOHNSON SPACE CENTER, HOUSTON "Do you read me, Houston?" When an astronaut contacts Earth, the Lyndon B. Johnson Space Center answers back. Here, twenty-five miles southeast of the city, lies NASA's center for human space exploration.

Inside a space helmet For practice, the astronaut puts on the suit that will be worn in space. The helmet has two microphones, a straw connected to an in-suit drink bag (containing thirty-two ounces of water), and a piece of foam rubber that the nose can push against to equalize pressure that may build up in the ears.

Neutral Buoyancy Laboratory To help astronauts prepare for microgravity, the Johnson Space Center has built the largest indoor pool in the world: 202 feet long, 102 feet wide, and 40 feet deep, holding 6.2 million gallons of water. In its near-weightless environment, astronauts rehearse the tasks they will later perform in space.

Mission Control Center Since 1965, Mission Control Center in Houston has been the nerve center for America's manned space programs. Here, flight controllers keep a twenty-four-hour vigil during space-shuttle flights. They also provide the expertise needed to deal with unexpected events.

OIL Texas is the nation's leading producer of oil. The industry developed in the eastern part of the state, but spread west after the discovery of the Permian Basin—an oil-rich, 200-million-year-old seafloor.

Midland-Odessa These oil pumps, or "grasshoppers," are between Midland and Odessa, headquarters for oil production in West Texas.

Port Arthur Refineries stretch for miles at the junction of two highways, State 82 and State 87 (just southeast of Port Arthur). This region, which also includes Beaumont and Orange, is touted as the world's largest petrochemical complex.

Port of Galveston Offshore drilling rigs are sometimes brought to shore for maintenance and repair. This view is from *Ocean Star*, an old rig that has been turned into a museum.

**State Reptile:
HORNED LIZARD**
COMMONLY KNOWN AS
HORNED TOAD

Port of Corpus Christi In terms of tonnage, Corpus Christi is the largest port in Texas after Houston. The water-level markings on this oil tanker indicate that it is presently carrying no cargo.

SHRIMP Shrimping is big business in Texas, accounting for about 80 percent of all commercial fishing.

Port Isabel These trawlers in Port Isabel (on the Gulf of Mexico, just south of Padre Island) are being prepared for another seagoing mission. The fishermen—many of whom are Vietnamese immigrants—often stay out for up to two months.

**State Musical Instrument:
GUITAR**

River Walk, San Antonio For feasting on gulf shrimp, the River Walk offers the perfect setting—an "underground" oasis right in the bustling commercial city center. Several stone staircases descend from the street to cobblestone or flagstone paths that extend almost three miles along the meandering San Antonio River. Restaurants and cafés line the way, sightseeing boats frequently glide by, and thirty-five bridges make crossing easy. The River Walk even has its own outdoor theater, with the river flowing between stage and audience.

WILDLIFE In Texas, it's not difficult to spot wild animals in their natural habitats. For particularly good viewing, there are thirteen national wildlife refuges and more than one hundred state and national parks. Of all bird species found in America, 75 percent can be sighted in Texas—

**State Sport:
RODEO**

State Insect:
MONARCH BUTTERFLY

and the "Great Texas Coast Birding Trail," a seven-hundred-mile driving tour, offers a unique opportunity to see most of them.

Coyote Considered a pest by ranchers, the coyote is viewed in American Indian tradition as a "trickster," a lover of pranks. It can be spotted all over the state, but is particularly common in south Texas brush country.

Roadrunner Other birds fly; this one runs, clocking in at about fifteen miles per hour. In TV-land it has "beep-beeped" its way to stardom; in Texas, where it is found especially in brush country, it is also known as a chaparral cock or paisano.

Whooping crane In 1941, there were only fifteen whooping cranes left in the wild. Now, more than 100 of these five-foot-tall white birds, with a wingspan of seven and a half feet, arrive every November at the Aransas National Wildlife Refuge. Their monthlong flight from Canada, where they spend the summer, covers 2,500 miles.

Javelina Common in Big Bend, this wild, tusked, piglike creature is actually more closely related to horses. Because it is nearsighted and naturally curious, it occasionally approaches people for a few sniffs.

Jackrabbit This creature's long ears can pick up sounds from great distances away, a necessity for an animal that is prey for coyotes, eagles, bobcats, and other predators. On hot days in the desert—where it is most commonly found—its ears also act as radiators, releasing extra body heat.

Tarantula This large, hairy inhabitant of the deserts of southern and West Texas may be fearsome to look at, but it is really quite harmless. It may bite in self-defense, but is not poisonous.

Cactus wren Texas has more than six hundred species of birds. The cactus nest of this southwest Texas bird is unique: a large domed structure, twelve inches in diameter, with a side entrance.

Kangaroo rat This rodent, which makes its home in the Trans-Peco area, is spotted mostly at night. It does not drink water; instead, it gathers moisture from seeds and from condensation in its nasal passages.

Trap-door spider This large, hairy spider digs a burrow and covers the entrance with a perfectly round, hinged lid. Periodically it will come out to drag in prey for dinner.

State Flag

Mexican free-tailed bat At sunset between April and October, 1.5 million squeaking Mexican free-tailed bats will take flight, darkening the sky. Having dined on some 30,000 pounds of bugs—their nightly consumption—the bats return to their roost under the Congress Avenue Bridge in Austin. The city even provides a "bat hotline" that alerts watchers of estimated flight times.

Alligator In the bayous of East Texas and in the marshes along the Gulf Coast live some 200,000 alligators. Though they look scary, no human fatality has ever been attributed to them in the state.

American bittern This large bird, living in marshes, uses amazing camouflage. Drawing its feathers in tightly and pointing its bill skyward, the bird melts into the vertical lights and shadows of marsh plants, swaying with the reeds.

THE RIO GRANDE From the Rocky Mountains, through Colorado and New Mexico, the Rio Grande flows into Texas and winds its way to the Gulf of Mexico. It forms a 1,270-mile boundary between Mexico and the United States. The border, or La Frontera (as the Mexicans call it), is more than a thin line separating two countries. It is a special environment in which two cultures merge.

State Gem:
TEXAS BLUE TOPAZ

El Camino del Rio El Camino del Rio (literally, river road) is a particularly scenic stretch along the Rio Grande between Presidio and Lajitas. Originally a trail used by Spanish explorers, it is now part of a road known as FM 170.

El Paso Twin cities are not uncommon along the Rio Grande. Opposite Laredo is Nuevo Laredo, and next to Brownsville, by the Gulf of Mexico, lies Matamoros. El Paso, tucked away in the westernmost corner of Texas, looks across the river to Juarez, Mexico's fourth-largest city.

Acknowledgments

Thanks to the folks at Lambshead Ranch, Albany; Mike Talley and Anne Cook at the Texas Department of Transportation; and to my husband, Bo Zaunders, for his help with the research. Thanks also to Laura Rochon, Johnson Space Center; Jane Jacobs, Top of Texas Rodeo; Adrian Witkosky, American Cotton Museum; Frank Smith, Antique Sewing Machine Museum; "Buddy" Rua, Mary Elizabeth Hopkins Santa Claus Museum; Joe Taylor, Mt. Blanco Fossil Museum; Dorinda Millan, West of the Pecos Museum; the Forestry Museum; the Devil's Rope Museum; Texas Hatters; J. L. Mercer; the *Ocean Star*; the Dallas Cowboys; and the Kimbell Art Museum.